E3011 20 August 1974

E3011 (81009) is seen at Birmingham New Street along with No. 85026. E3011 had yet to receive its TOPS number of 81009, and it would not gain it until 1975. E3011 would eventually be scrapped along with many of its classmates by Coopers Metals, Attercliffe, in 1992.

03089 21 April 1984

No. 03089 (D2089) is seen at York stabling point, complete with match wagon, and also surrounded by Class 08 shunters. No. 03089 would eventually find its way into preservation, and can today be found at Mangapps Railway Museum.

03119 15 June 1980

No. 03119 (D2119) is seen resting for the weekend at Llanelli shed in South Wales. This was one of the Class 03 locomotives that received a cut-down cab for working on the Burry Port & Gwendreath Valley line. No. 03119 was eventually preserved and is today working at the Epping & Ongar Railway.

03142 2 May 1976

No. 03142 (D2142) is seen again, stabled at Llanelli shed in the company of classmate No. 03120. Both of these locomotives had cut-down cabs, and would eventually be replaced by cut-down Class 08/9 locomotives. No. 03142 was scrapped at Swindon Works in 1985.

BR BLUE IN THE 1970S AND 1980S

Andrew Cole

AMBERLEY

First published 2017

Amberley Publishing
The Hill, Stroud
Gloucestershire, GL5 4EP

www.amberley-books.com

Copyright © Andrew Cole, 2017

The right of Andrew Cole to be identified as
the Author of this work has been asserted in
accordance with the Copyrights, Designs and
Patents Act 1988.

ISBN 978 1 4456 7402 5 (print)
ISBN 978 1 4456 7403 2 (ebook)

British Library Cataloguing in Publication Data.
A catalogue record for this book is available from
the British Library.

Origination by Amberley Publishing.
Printed in the UK.

Introduction

When British Rail was formed in 1948, it inherited a whole host of different-liveried locomotives and stock from the former pre-nationalised companies. In the early 1960s it was decided to have a new corporate image for the whole of the fleet, to replace the BR green livery.

An early predecessor was D1733, which was painted in XP64 blue livery – a livery not too far off what was to become the standard livery for locomotives. An experimental rake of carriages was also painted into a new livery of blue and grey. The livery carried by the carriages would go on to become standard for the majority of DMU and EMU cars, and also for the carriage fleet. Despite this, some of the older EMU and DMU cars would be withdrawn carrying all-over blue livery, rather than the blue and grey.

The livery on the Class 47 was slightly changed to a darker shade of blue, and from 1965 onwards locomotives began appearing in the new livery, replacing the mainly BR green livery. At the time, the locomotives still carried their pre-TOPS numbering – the renumbering not being implemented until the early 1970s – so it was more than possible to see blue-liveried locomotives with pre-TOPS numbers.

BR blue would be rolled out across nearly the entire fleet, although there were some locomotives that were withdrawn still carrying their old liveries, the most notable being the Class 42 'Warships'.

There was one notable exception, this being No. 40106, which would be the last locomotive running on British Rail that carried the old green livery. As such, when it was due for repainting, it received a fresh coat of green, with the loco never carrying blue livery in its entire life, even in preservation.

With the vast majority of the fleet carrying blue livery, certain depots decided to personalise their allocation, with the most notable being Stratford in East London, who painted a silver roof onto their Class 47s, and also onto a couple of Class 31s. Finsbury Park, also in London, applied white window surrounds to their Class 55 allocation, and Old Oak Common applied white stripes to their Class 31/4s.

The first change from standard blue came when No. 56036 was experimentally applied with large logo livery. This would eventually become the new standard livery, with both freight and passenger locomotives receiving this livery, and the Class 56s receiving it from 1980 onwards.

The next major change would see passenger locomotives receiving InterCity livery from 1983 onwards. The freight locomotives would then start to be repainted into Railfreight grey, with the Class 58s introduced in this livery from 1983 onwards.

BR blue provided a very uniform livery for the entire fleet during the 1970s and early 1980s, with large numbers of locomotives eventually being withdrawn and scrapped carrying the livery, and indeed it has proved a popular livery for preserved lines to repaint their locomotives and stock.

I hope you enjoy looking through this album of my late father's photographs, and hopefully it will bring back some happy memories as it has done for me in compiling it. I would like to dedicate this book to the memory of my late father, Anthony Cole, who introduced my brother and I to this hobby.

49 17 July 1974

No. 49 (45039) approaches Water Orton station from the Leicester direction with a rake of loaded mineral wagons while on a Class 9 working. No. 49 carries the name *The Manchester Regiment*, and has lost the 'D' prefix from its number following the end of steam. No. 49 was renumbered 45039 and was an early withdrawal, being scrapped at Swindon Works in 1983.

54 20 August 1974

No. 54 (45023) *The Royal Pioneer Corps* is seen during the summer of 1974 at Birmingham New Street with a Class 1 passenger working. The steam heat is working well, and also of note are the postal Brutes on the platform – a sight now sadly missing from today's railways. No. 54 was renumbered 45023 and was scrapped by Vic Berry, Leicester, in 1986.

1723 26 October 1972

No. 1723 (47540, 47975) is seen at Tyseley, Birmingham, running light engine. No. 1723 carries BR blue livery, but also carries two British Rail double arrows and has its running number on both cabsides. After various renumberings, this loco would be withdrawn carrying the number 47540, and was scrapped by T. J. Thompson, Stockton, in 2016.

6926 20 September 1973

No. 6926 (37226, 37379) passes through Water Orton station with a Class 6 oil working. The load consists of a rake of shiny two-axle tank wagons. No. 6926 had lost its 'D' prefix by this time, and would eventually be renumbered 37379, being scrapped by C. F. Booths, Rotherham, in 2008.

7631 20 September 1973

No. 7631 (25281) passes through Water Orton with a mixed Class 8 freight working. Today, over forty years later, this view has changed little; the exception being that the fourth track over on the left-hand side has been lifted. No. 7631 was renumbered 25281, and was scrapped at Swindon Works in 1981.

D1013 2 May 1976

D1013 *Western Ranger* is seen stabled at Landore depot, Swansea. The Western class of locomotives had less than twelve months' service life in them when this shot was taken, with the class being officially withdrawn in February 1977. D1013 would be saved for preservation, and can today be found at the Severn Valley Railway.

D1047 20 August 1974

D1047 is seen arriving at Birmingham New Street with a passenger working from London Paddington. This loco carries the name *Western Lord*, and it would be scrapped at Swindon Works in 1976.

D1054 2 May 1976

D1054 *Western Governor* is seen stabled at Gloucester in company with a Class 45 'Peak' locomotive. This class of locomotive was in decline at the time of this shot, and D1054 would be withdrawn just six months later, being scrapped at Swindon Works in 1977.

03149 27 July 1980

No. 03149 (D2149) is seen stabled around the side of Lincoln shed. At this time, a number of Class 03s were allocated to Lincoln for shunting at the depot. No. 03149 was withdrawn just two years later and was scrapped at Doncaster Works in 1983.

03151 2 May 1976

No. 03151 (D2151) rests for the weekend at Landore depot, Swansea. This was another cut-down example, as was No. 03145, coupled behind. The height difference can be seen when compared to the full-height Class 08 behind. No. 03151 was scrapped by C. F. Booth, Rotherham, in 1985.

03152 15 June 1980

No. 03152 (D2152) is seen stabled at Llanelli depot, having not long been released from works overhaul. The Class 03s were allocated to South Wales mainly for coal workings on the Burry Port & Gwendreath Valley line, and all had to have cut-down cabs fitted due to low bridges on the line. No. 03152 was saved for preservation and can today be found at the Swindon & Cricklade Railway.

03158 22 March 1981

No. 03158 (D2158) is seen stabled at Norwich, complete with match wagon. These wagons were coupled to the Class 03s to help activate the track circuits. No. 03158 was another Class 03 to be preserved, and it can be found today at Titley Junction, Herefordshire.

03168 13 April 1980

No. 03168 (D2168) is seen stabled outside the impressive Stratford depot, East London. This depot was huge and had a very large allocation of main line and shunting locomotives. Sadly it has since been closed and demolished, making way for the Olympic Stadium. No. 03168 didn't fare much better, being scrapped at Doncaster Works in 1982.

03196 22 March 1981

No. 03196 (D2196) is seen stabled for the weekend at Ipswich. This loco is also coupled to a match wagon to assist with track circuits. No. 03196 was preserved, and can today be found at Steamtown, Carnforth.

03389 27 July 1980

No. 03389 (D2389) spends the weekend stabled outside Lincoln shed, along with classmate No. 03149 and a host of first generation DMU cars. No. 03389 would eventually be scrapped by C. F. Booth, Rotherham, in 1983.

03397 22 March 1981

No. 03397 (D2397) is seen acting as station pilot at Norwich. Today all the buildings in the background have been demolished, and also of note are the former fish wagons and departmental stock in the background. No. 03397 was scrapped by Vic Berry, Leicester, in 1991.

07005 3 April 1976

No. 07005 (D2989) is seen stabled at Eastleigh depot. This class of loco were all based on the Southern Region, being initially used on the tight track at Southampton Docks. No. 07005 would enter preservation, and can today be found at Boden Rail, Washwood Heath.

08051 28 July 1984

No. 08051 (13064, D3064) stands condemned at Tinsley depot, Sheffield. This loco had been withdrawn two years previous, and would be sent to Swindon Works for final scrapping, which occurred in 1986.

08499 20 April 1984

No. 08499 (D3654) is seen stabled at York stabling point, in typical condition of the early 1980s, carrying standard BR blue livery, and is complete with shunter's pole on the front steps. No. 08499 is still active today, based at Cardiff Canton working for Pullman Rail.

09002 3 April 1976

No. 09002 (D3666) is seen stabled at Brighton. The Class 09s had a different gear ratio when compared to the Class 08s, and they also had a higher top speed. The majority of the class were also fitted with high-level air pipes, as they were used mainly on the Southern Region. No. 09002 is still in use today, working at Whitemoor Yard, March.

09009 23 July 1985

No. 09009 (D3720) is seen at Clapham Junction acting as yard pilot. The Class 09s were based at Clapham to shunt the parcels vans, and also any Southern Region third rail EMUs. No. 09009 carries the waist-high air pipes that most members of the class had fitted. Today No. 09009 can be found working at Whitemoor Yard, March.

13002 16 February 1980

No. 13002 (D4502) is seen stabled at its home depot of Tinsley, Sheffield. There were just three of these locomotives in use with British Rail, all based at Tinsley for shunting the hump yard. The loco was converted from two Class 08 locomotives, D4187 and D3697, becoming a master and slave loco. No. 13002 was the first of the class to be withdrawn, and was scrapped at Swindon Works in 1982.

20040 24 February 1980

No. 20040 (D8040) is seen stabled at Saltley depot, Birmingham. At this time, the loco's BR symbol was still located on the cabside, and had yet to be moved to just behind the cab. No. 20040 was eventually withdrawn and sold to RFS Engineering for use as a source of spare parts for their Channel Tunnel construction Class 20s, and No. 20040 was scrapped by MC Metals, Glasgow, in 1992.

20069 24 February 1980

No. 20069 (D8069) is seen, also stabled at Saltley depot, Birmingham surrounded by many other classmates. No. 20069 was one of the lucky class members, being saved for preservation, and can today be found working at the Mid Norfolk Railway.

20073 17 May 1981

No. 20073 (D8073) rests at Saltley depot, Birmingham. By this time the BR double arrow symbol had been moved to behind the locomotive cab, and the headcode discs on the front of the loco had been removed, except for the one between the cab windows. No. 20073 would eventually be scrapped by C. F. Booth, Rotherham, in 2006.

20192 18 June 1980

No. 20192 (D8192) is seen stabled at Saltley depot, Birmingham, in front of the depot admin building. Of note are the old departmental coaches to the right. No. 20192 would eventually be scrapped by MC Metals, Glasgow, in 1991.

24005 14 March 1976

No. 24005 (D5000) is seen withdrawn at Reddish depot. This loco was the pioneer Class 24 locomotive, delivered new as D5000 in 1958. A candidate for preservation, it was not to be, and No. 24005 was scrapped at Swindon Works in 1977.

24020 14 March 1976

No. 24020 (D5020) is seen, also at Reddish depot, and this too had been withdrawn the year previous. Of note, is the fact that No. 24020 still retains its pre-TOPS number of 5020 on the secondman's cab. No. 24020 would eventually be scrapped at Swindon Works in 1977.

24101 22 February 1976

No. 24101 (D5101) is seen on the arrival roads at Doncaster Works along with classmate No. 24100. Both of these Scottish locomotives had been withdrawn at the start of the month, moving south for scrapping at Doncaster, which was to be in March 1976 for No. 24101, and in May 1976 for No. 24100.

25027 20 January 1980

No. 25027 (D5177) is seen stabled at Saltley depot, Birmingham, complete with a full set of miniature snowploughs attached. This loco would be withdrawn in May 1983, and would spend the next two years dumped on Saltley awaiting its fate. It was eventually sent to Swindon Works, but with the works due to close, the scrapping of locos had ceased. No. 25027 was then sold to Vic Berry, Leicester, who cut the loco in 1987.

25087 25 July 1975

No. 25087 (D5237) is seen stabled on one of the through roads at Birmingham New Street, complete with a rake of MkI carriages. The summer months at Birmingham New Street used to attract a whole host of loco hauled workings on summer Saturday extras, something that nowadays doesn't happen. No. 25087 was allocated to the Scottish region at the time, and was eventually scrapped at Swindon Works in 1981.

25089 8 February 1981

No. 25089 (D5239) is seen having just been refuelled at Springs Branch depot, Wigan. At this time there were still many Class 25s in use, mainly on freight workings. No. 25089 would survive in service up until 1986, but was eventually scrapped by Vic Berry, Leicester, in 1987.

25120 19 July 1975

No. 25120 (D5270) is seen ready to depart from Birmingham New Street while working double-headed with a classmate on a Class 1 passenger working. During the summer months at this time, British Rail used to have summer Saturday extras, which could be hauled by almost any available traction. No. 25120 would eventually be scrapped at Swindon Works in 1984.

25148 1 June 1981

No. 25148 (D5298) is seen stabled at Nuneaton awaiting its next turn of duty. The impressive building in the background has since been demolished, and No. 25148 was scrapped at Swindon Works in 1983 following collision damage.

25161 12 August 1976

No. 25161 (D7511) is seen running light engine through Rhyl station during the scorching-hot summer of 1976. The Class 25 locomotives were equally at home working light passenger trains as well as freight moves. No. 25161 would be scrapped by Vic Berry, Leicester, in 1988.

25173 31 August 1984

No. 25173 (D7523) is seen at the south end of Crewe station, having just been refuelled, and was preparing to stable. At this time there were still plenty of Class 25 locomotives in use, with their eventual withdrawal from British Rail not happening until 1987. No. 25173 was saved for preservation, and can today be found at the Epping & Ongar Railway.

25182 25 February 1984

No. 25182 (D7532) rests for the weekend at Cockshute Sidings, Stoke-on-Trent. This was a busy little stabling point, with not only locomotives stabled, but also Midland Region EMUs and DMUs. No. 25182 was eventually scrapped at Swindon Works in 1985.

25185 13 April 1985

No. 25185 (D7535) is seen stabled at Toton depot, Nottinghamshire. By this time, No. 25185 had been withdrawn from service, and had been sold to the Dart Valley Railway for preservation. It would later move to Paignton where the loco is still in use today. No. 25185 carries its pre-TOPS number of D7535 under the secondman's cabside window.

25198 9 March 1980

No. 25198 (D7548) is seen stabled outside the shed at Northwich depot, Cheshire. No. 25198 is complete with a set of miniature snowploughs attached, and it would be scrapped by Vic Berry, Leicester, in 1987.

25219 23 May 1982

No. 25219 (D7569) is seen stabled at Cockshute Sidings, Stoke-on-Trent, along with classmate No. 25160. At this time, No. 25219 still carried a set of roller blinds, not yet having them plated over with the domino panel. No. 25219 was eventually scrapped at Swindon Works in 1987.

25226 26 October 1980

No. 25226 (D7576) is seen stabled at Polmadie depot, Glasgow. This loco shows signs of being overhauled at St Rollox Works, with the larger than normal numerals applied. No. 25226 was scrapped at Doncaster Works in 1986.

25261 22 November 1981

No. 25261 (D7611) stands condemned at Tyseley depot, Birmingham. This loco still carries the tablet-catching recess underneath the driver's cabside window, with its running number applied on the bodyside. No. 25261 was dumped at Tyseley for around twelve months before moving to Derby Works for scrapping, which took around two years from start to eventual finish in 1985.

25283 20 February 1985

No. 25283 (D7633, 25904) passes through Nuneaton station with a short engineers train, consisting of a single van, a mess coach and a crane. No. 25283 was renumbered as 25904 later in its career for freight working in the North West. It was saved for preservation, and can today be found at the Dean Forest Railway.

26031 26 October 1980

No. 26031 (D5331) is seen outside Eastfield depot, Glasgow, having recently been overhauled and repainted at the nearby St Rollox Works. No. 26031 is complete with a full set of miniature snowploughs attached, and would eventually be scrapped by MC Metals, Glasgow, in 1991, having suffered fire damage.

27014 5 June 1983

No. 27014 (D5360) is seen on display at Coalville open day 1983. This loco had been at Derby Works for overhaul, and was sent to Coalville for display before returning north. It is seen with a full set of miniature snowploughs added, and also carries its running number on the cabside, which is where Derby applied them, instead of on the bodyside. No. 27014 would return to the Midlands for scrapping, being disposed of by Vic Berry, Leicester, in 1987.

27204 26 October 1980

No. 27204 (D5403, 27122, 27058) is seen stabled for the weekend outside Eastfield depot, Glasgow. The Class 27/2 sub-class were used on top and tail passenger workings between Glasgow and Edinburgh. No. 27204 was eventually renumbered No. 27058 when it had been replaced on the passenger working by Class 47/7 locos, and was scrapped by Vic Berry, Leicester, in 1987.

27211 26 October 1980

No. 27211 (D5411, 27117, 27065) is seen stabled outside Eastfield depot, Glasgow. This was another loco that had just been released from overhaul at the nearby St Rollox Works, the loco's BR blue livery still shining. No. 27211 was eventually renumbered 27065, and would be another loco sent south to Leicester for scrapping, with Vic Berry completing the work in 1987.

31183 29 May 1980

No. 31183 (D5604) stands at Saltley depot, Birmingham in front of the depot's re-railing coaches. This scene was to change very little over the years, but the track on which the Class 31 stands was lifted, along with the track adjacent to the Class 47. The depot closed in 2009 and all the buildings were demolished.

31230 13 April 1980

No. 31230 (D5657) stands outside the famous factory at Old Oak Common depot, West London. The loco is standing on one of the turntable roads, with the turntable an unusual feature for a diesel depot. Today, sadly, this large depot has been demolished, making way for the new Crossrail depot and sidings.

31264 6 December 1983

No. 31264 (D5694) is seen on the lines adjacent to Lawley Street container terminal near Saltley, Birmingham. The main depot can be seen in the background, and is the other side of the Birmingham to Derby main line. No. 31264 would eventually be scrapped by MC Metals, Glasgow, in 1995.

31401 13 August 1982

No. 31401 (D5589) is seen departing Bristol Temple Meads along with classmate No. 31420, this being the standard corporate image of the time, with all-over blue locos and blue and grey carriages. No. 31401 would be withdrawn following collision damage, and would be scrapped at Doncaster Works in 1988.

31407 3 April 1985

No. 31407 (D5640, 31507) is seen departing Nuneaton with a passenger working for Birmingham New Street. This was a typical working of the time, being loco-hauled from Norwich to Birmingham; often producing an ETH-fitted Class 31. No. 31407 shows the remains of the bodyside white stripe that was applied to certain members of the Class. No. 31407 would be scrapped by Ron Hull, Rotherham, in 2006.

31423 11 August 1984

No. 31423 (D5621, 31197) is seen passing Saltley depot, Birmingham, working in tandem with classmate No. 31416. Summer Saturdays used to produce a pair of Class 31s on the dinnertime arrival from Norwich, however they were to be replaced eventually by a Stratford-based Class 47. No. 31423 would be scrapped by T. J Thompson, Stockton, in 2009.

33008 6 September 1980

No. 33008 (D6508) *Eastleigh* is seen stabled at Basingstoke, coupled to a rake of parcels vans. This loco would go on to receive a repaint back into BR green livery within a few years, and it would eventually be preserved. It can today be found on the Battlefield Line, Shackerstone.

33020 23 July 1985

No. 33020 (D6537) is seen passing through Clapham Junction with a parcels working. At this time there used to be a large amount of parcels traffic on the network, but it has all since been lost. No. 33020 would be scrapped at Stewarts Lane in 1997.

33033 23 July 1985

No. 33033 (D6551) passes through Clapham Junction with a parcels working, heading for one of the London terminals. No. 33033 would eventually be another member of the class to be scrapped at Stewarts Lane in 1997.

33057 13 August 1982

No. 33057 (D6575) runs light engine into Bristol Temple Meads, ready to take up a passenger working. This class were common visitors to Bristol at this time, with workings through to Westbury and Portsmouth. No. 33057 would be saved for preservation, and can today be found working at the West Somerset Railway.

33065 4 April 1976

No. 33065 (D6585) is seen stabled outside the shed at Hither Green depot, London. Of note are the red departmental carriages, as well as the crane that can just be glimpsed inside the shed. No. 33065 was successfully preserved, and can today be found at the Spa Valley Railway.

37018 27 July 1980

No. 37018 (D6718, 37517) is seen stabled at Immingham depot, in front of the redundant coal stage. The loco shares siding space with classmate No. 37126. No. 37018 would eventually be rebuilt as No. 37517; it is today used as a source of spares at Carnforth for the West Coast Railways fleet.

37040 27 July 1980

No. 37040 (D6740) is seen stabled in the summer sun at Goole Docks along with various other classmates, including No. 37249. Of note is the fact that neither of the Class 37s have yet to have the skirting removed from the front of the loco, something that the majority of the class had removed. No. 37040 was scrapped by C. F. Booth, Rotherham, in 2006.

37080 12 September 1978

No. 37080 (D6780) passes through Bescot in near-original condition, the only change being the livery and the headcode blinds exchanged for dots. Bescot used to be a major hive of activity at this time, with a vast number of locos passing through, and also stabling, particularly of a weekend. No. 37080 would be scrapped at Cardiff Canton in 1997.

37096 24 August 1983

No. 37096 (D6796) is seen passing through Platform 1 at Doncaster. This loco is seen on test, having been through the nearby works for overhaul, as it is hauling the works' test train. The overhaul included a repaint into standard blue livery, which was the norm at this time. No. 37096 was an early withdrawal for the class, and was scrapped by MC Metals, Glasgow, in 1991.

37176 2 May 1976

No. 37176 (D6876, 37883) spends the weekend stabled at Margam depot, South Wales. This class of locomotive was synonymous with South Wales freight workings throughout their careers, until replaced by the Class 66s. No. 37176 would be selected to be refurbished and was rebuilt as No. 37883, eventually being sent to Spain for high-speed line construction workings.

37179 8 June 1980

No. 37179 (D6879, 37691, 37612) is seen stabled at Swindon along with a brake van. This loco went through a couple of renumberings in its life, firstly being rebuilt as No. 37691, and then as No. 37612 when it was in use with EPS.

37185 10 February 1980

No. 37185 (D6885) is seen stabled on Saltley depot, Birmingham looking superb with a full set of miniature snowploughs attached. Despite the class visiting Saltley, they were never as common as other classes during this time, with No. 37185 being based at Cardiff Canton at the time. No. 37185 was scrapped by Booth Roe Metals, Rotherham, in 2006.

37232 2 May 1976

No. 37232 (D6932) is seen stabled at Swansea East Dock, in company with another classmate. Class 37s were used heavily in South Wales on coal, steel and, most famously, triple-headed on the iron ore workings to Llanwern. No. 37232 would not be chosen to be refurbished, and was scrapped at Wigan CRDC, by EWS, in 2000.

37286 2 May 1976

No. 37286 (D6986, 37404) is seen stabled for the weekend at Aberdare. The loco is seen with a brake van attached to either end of the loco. This loco spent many years based in South Wales, before being refurbished as No. 37404 and fitted with ETH equipment and being sent to Scotland for passenger workings. As No. 37404, this loco was scrapped by Booth Roe Metals, Rotherham, in 2002.

37299 2 May 1976

No. 37299 (D6999, 37426) is seen stabled at Barry, South Wales, complete with headcode blinds wound back to 0000, as they were no longer in use. The headcode panels would eventually be plated over, and marker lights fitted. No. 37299 was eventually rebuilt as ETH-fitted No. 37426.

40001 14 March 1976

No. 40001 (D201) is seen stabled at Springs Branch depot, Wigan. This was one of the major depots in the North West, with a large allocation at the time, and is still standing today, although it was later used for spares recovery and the scrapping of EWS locos. No. 40001 was eventually scrapped at Swindon Works in 1987.

40012 24 August 1983

No. 40012 (D212, 97407) stands at Doncaster, awaiting the road with a parcels working. This was a Cleethorpes to Longsight working, and No. 40012 was allocated to Kingmoor depot Carlisle at the time. No. 40012 carries the name *Aureol*, although the original cast name has been removed, and a painted one is seen in its place. No. 40012 was selected to be renumbered No. 97407, and was used in the Crewe station remodelling in 1985. It was eventually saved for preservation, and is today at Barrow Hill.

40018 14 March 1976

No. 40018 (D218) is seen stabled at Edge Hill depot, Liverpool, along with a classmate and a Class 25. No. 40018 was originally named *Carmania*, but by this time had lost the plates. No. 40018 was scrapped at Crewe Works in 1983.

40020 12 August 1976

No. 40020 (D220) passes light engine through Rhyl station in the hot summer of '76. No. 40020 was another member of the class that was named, being named *Franconia*, but again by this time the plates had been removed. No. 40020 was another Class 40 scrapped at Crewe Works, this time in 1987.

40047 2 April 1983

No. 40047 (D247) is seen stabled at Cockshute Sidings, Stoke-on-Trent. There was always a good variety of loco to be found at these sidings, from Class 20s to Class 25s and also Class 47s. There also used to be DMUs and EMUs stabled on the carriage sidings as well. No. 40047 was eventually scrapped at Doncaster Works in 1986.

40069 7 April 1981

No. 40069 (D269) is seen stabled at Saltley depot, Birmingham, along with a good selection of other types of blue liveried traction, including a large logo liveried Class 56. No. 40069 was unique in the Class 40 fleet, as it had the bottom few inches of bodywork cut away to expose the pipework, and this remained the only loco treated in this way. No. 40069 was scrapped at Doncaster Works in 1984.

40069 24 August 1983

No. 40069 (D269) pauses at Doncaster while hauling a rake of two-axle tank wagons. This view shows more clearly the few inches of bodywork that have been cut away from the bottom of the loco, revealing the pipework. No. 40069 only had one more month of service ahead of it, being withdrawn in the September.

40088 12 August 1976

No. 40088 (D288) is seen making a station call at Rhyl on a glorious summer's day with a rake of Mk1 carriages. This was the year of record temperatures, and drought condition in the United Kingdom. No. 40088 would go on to be scrapped at Crewe Works in 1988; however, one cab was saved for preservation, and it can today be found at the Railway Age, Crewe.

40093 6 April 1982

No. 40093 (D293) is seen departing Lawley Street container terminal, Birmingham with a loaded working. At this time, Saltley depot used to turn out any available loco for these container workings, from Class 25s, through to Class 50s and also later on Class 58s. No. 40093 would be scrapped at Doncaster Works in 1984.

40104 31 August 1984

No. 40104 (D304) departs Crewe with a passenger working from Birmingham New Street to Llandudno. Of note is the fact that the first carriage is a First Class Mk1 vehicle, possibly declassified for the trip. At this time the Class 40 locomotives were in serious decline, and the last one was taken out of traffic in January 1985, except for celebrity D200, which had been reinstated carrying BR green livery. No. 40104 was eventually scrapped at Crewe Works in 1988.

40133 26 October 1982

No. 40133 (D333) is seen stabled at Nuneaton. The Class 40s had three different front-end designs, with the split headcode boxes being carried by only twenty members of the class. No. 40133 would be scrapped at Doncaster Works in 1984.

40137 13 January 1980

No. 40137 (D337) is seen stabled in the early morning sunshine at Cockshute Sidings, Stoke-on-Trent. This view shows the enormous size of these locomotives, with a locomotive weighing in at 136 tonnes. No. 40137 would eventually be scrapped at Swindon Works in 1981.

40175 12 August 1976

No. 40175 (D375) passes straight through Rhyl station with a passenger working consisting of solely Mk1 carriages. No. 40175 has had its headcode blinds wound back to 0000, as they were no longer required by the signallers to identify the working. No. 40175 was scrapped at Swindon Works in 1983.

40177 12 August 1976

No. 40177 (D377) passes beneath the impressive number 2 signal box at Rhyl with a loaded ballast working from Penmaenmawr. This signal box is still standing today at Rhyl, as it is a listed building, although it was taken out of use in 1990. No. 40177 was scrapped at Crewe Works in 1986.

40177 5 June 1983

No. 40177 (D377) is seen on display at Coalville open day 1983. Despite only having a small space for display, these open days at Coalville used to be superb, with plenty of variety on show. No. 40177 shows signs of being spruced up for the event, including white buffers and red bufferbeams, with just the remains of its pre-TOPS number, 377, also on the bodyside.

40181 27 January 1980

No. 40181 (D381) is seen stabled on Saltley depot, Birmingham, waiting its next turn of service. In the background can be seen the re-railing carriages, and also a snowplough, with a Class 37 and a Class 47 in attendance. No. 40181 was scrapped at Crewe Works in 1986.

40183 13 January 1980

No. 40183 (D383) is seen at Crewe Works having just emerged from the paint shop following a repaint during an overhaul. The Class 40s were synonymous with the Crewe area, with the depot having a large allocation, and also the works overhauling, and eventually scrapping, a vast number of the class. No. 40183 would be one of those scrapped at Crewe, in 1986.

40188 31 May 1981

No. 40188 (D388) stands on display at Coalville open day 1981. This is one of my earliest train-related memories, as both of the remaining Class 44 locomotives were also on display on the day. No. 40188 would eventually be scrapped at Crewe Works in 1984.

43132 30 November 1983

No. 43132 passes Saltley depot, Birmingham, while on a test run from Derby Works. These power cars had only been in service for four years, and yet had received their first overhaul. The test run running back to back was a common sight at the time. It is running with No. 43131.

43152 31 May 1981

No. 43152 is seen on display at Coalville open day 1981. This power car had only just been released from Crewe Works following construction, and had yet to enter service; it would be another fortnight before it was delivered to Old Oak Common.

44007 6 May 1974

No. 44007 *Ingleborough* is seen running light engine through Derby station with just a single brake van in tow. The Class 44s dated from 1959, and were the forerunners to a large fleet of Class 45 and Class 46 locomotives.

44007 17 May 1980

No. 44007 (D7) spends the weekend stabled at Toton depot, Nottinghamshire. There were only ten Class 44 locomotives, and they spent their entire lives allocated to Toton. No. 44007 was one of the last three in service, but whereas the other two were preserved, No. 44007 would not be so lucky, and it was scrapped at Derby Works in 1981 – the last Class 44 to be scrapped.

44008 12 September 1978

No. 44008 (D8) is seen departing from Bescot with a freight working. By this time, No. 44008 had lost its *Penyghent* nameplates, but had gained a second running number on the bodyside. Being one of the last three members of this class in service, No. 44008 would receive a fresh coat of BR blue livery and would be saved for preservation, today working at Peak Rail.

44009 5 August 1974

No. 44009 (D9) *Snowdon* is seen at Birmingham New Street having arrived on a passenger working. The Class 44s were rare on passenger turns, being mainly used on freight workings. No. 44009 had different grills on the side along with No. 44010, and the pair were instantly recognisable. No. 44009 was scrapped at Derby Works in 1980.

45007 24 February 1980

No. 45007 (D119) is seen stabled on Tyseley depot, Birmingham. Tyseley didn't have an allocation of main line diesels, although they did carry out repairs when required, as it was the main depot for the West Midlands DMU fleet. No. 45007 was eventually scrapped by MC Metals, Glasgow, in 1992.

45016 13 April 1985

No. 45016 (D16) is seen stabled at Toton in abysmal external condition, but the running number and front end have been cleaned. No. 45016 would only last in service for another seven months, and was scrapped by Vic Berry, Leicester, in 1986.

45017 6 May 1974

No. 45017 (D23, 968024) is seen waiting to depart from Derby station with a passenger working. No. 45017 had not long been released from works overhaul, which included a repaint into BR blue livery. Also of note is the fact the loco still retains split headcode boxes. No. 45017 would go on to be renumbered 968024 in the departmental fleet, but it was scrapped by MC Metals, Glasgow, in 1991.

45042 27 June 1983

No. 45042 (D57) is seen waiting to depart from Lawley Street container terminal with a loaded working. No. 45042 would lead an uneventful life and be scrapped by Vic Berry, Leicester, in 1986.

45053 1 June 1981

No. 45053 (D76) runs through Nuneaton with a loaded container working. No. 45053 still retains it split headcode boxes in this view, and indeed it would retain them right up until it was scrapped at Crewe Works in 1988, being the last member of the class to carry them.

45063 21 June 1983

No. 45063 (D104) is seen passing Water Orton with a freight working. Today this junction has been simplified, with the line to the left heading towards Derby, and the line behind the loco heading towards Nuneaton. No. 45063 was scrapped Vic Berry, Leicester, in 1988.

45111 15 November 1983

No. 45111 (D65) is seen arriving on the lines adjacent to Lawley Street container terminal with a rake of empty Freightliner container flat wagons. No. 45111 still retains its *Grenadier Guardsman* nameplates in this shot, although it has lost the crest. No. 45111 was eventually scrapped by MC Metals, Glasgow, in 1992.

45118 2 November 1983

No. 45118 (D67) *The Royal Artilleryman* is seen stabled outside the admin building at Saltley depot, Birmingham. Saltley always attracted a large amount of locos for servicing due to its central location and the vast amount of traffic generated in the area. No. 45118 was preserved, and can today be found at Loram, Derby.

46004 25 July 1975

No. 46004 (D141) is seen at Birmingham New Street waiting to depart with 1E75, an express working to the North East. New Street was always a busy place to spend a day, with workings requiring an engine change from electric to diesel and vice versa. No. 46004 would be scrapped at Swindon Works in 1985.

46027 13 August 1982

No. 46027 (D164) is seen at Bristol Temple Meads backing onto a passenger working for the North East. The 'Peak' classes of locomotives were synonymous with the North East to South West passenger workings at this time, until the new high-speed trains replaced them. No. 46027 was withdrawn on the last day of Class 46 operation, 25 November 1984, and it would be scrapped by Vic Berry, Leicester, in 1986.

46037 3 April 1982

No. 46037 (D174) is seen stabled at Saltley depot, Birmingham. This particular Class 46 was to retain its domino headcode panel right up until withdrawal, having caught fire at Kings Norton in 1984. It was later scrapped at Doncaster Works in 1985.

46044 10 February 1980

No. 46044 (D181) stands waiting its next turn of duty at Saltley depot, Birmingham. This was always a very hard depot to gain access to, only being granted visits very rarely. No. 46044 was another locomotive scrapped by Vic Berry, this time in 1986.

46048 31 May 1981

No. 46048 (D185) is seen on display at Coalville open day 1981. The cab on this loco was open for visits, something that was being taken advantage of at the time. No. 46048 would only last in service for another four months, being withdrawn with fire damage received at Gloucester. It was scrapped at Swindon Works in 1983.

46049 20 August 1974

No. 46049 (D186) is seen at Birmingham New Street with another North East-bound express working. The train consists of a rake of Mk1 carriages, and would have originated in the South West. Today these workings are operated by Cross Country Trains, using Voyager units. No. 46049 was eventually scrapped at Swindon Works in 1985.

46052 27 June 1983

No. 46052 (D189) is seen running light engine out of Lawley Street container terminal. Compared to the Class 45s, the Class 46s were withdrawn from traffic relatively early, all being withdrawn by 1984. No. 46052 only had another three months' service life left, and was scrapped at Doncaster Works in 1986.

47014 17 May 1980

No. 47014 (D1543) is seen stabled outside Toton depot, Nottinghamshire. This loco was allocated to Stratford depot, East London, at the time – the tell-tale sign being the silver roof. No. 47014 would eventually be scrapped by Booth Roe Metals, Rotherham, in 1992.

47019 22 March 1981

No. 47019 (D1573) is seen waiting to depart from Ipswich with a passenger working to London Liverpool Street. Of note is the trademark Stratford silver roof, and also the operational steam heating. No. 47019 was eventually scrapped in 1997 at Eastleigh.

47076 27 January 1980

No. 47076 (D1660, 47625, 47749) is seen at Saltley depot, Birmingham, awaiting its next turn of duty. This was one of the original Western Region named Class 47s, and it still carries its *City of Truro* plates. Amazingly, nearly forty years later this loco still carries this name, although it is now numbered 47749 in the Colas Rail Freight fleet.

47083 2 May 1976

No. 47083 (D1668, 47633) *Orion* is seen stabled at Landore depot, Swansea. Another of the original Western Region named Class 47s, this would go on to be refurbished at Crewe, emerging as No. 47633, but it was eventually scrapped by MC Metals, Glasgow, in 1994.

47089 2 May 1976

No. 47089 (D1675) spends the weekend stabled at Cardiff Canton depot. No. 47089 carries the name *Amazon*, with this batch of Class 47s named in the 1960s. This loco spent its entire life allocated to the Western Region, until it was withdrawn with collision damage it received at Chinley in 1987. It was later scrapped by Coopers Metals, Sheffield, in 1989.

47100 20 February 1985

No. 47100 (D1687) is seen stabled in the snow at Nuneaton. This class of loco represented the largest class in the British Rail main-line fleet at the time, totalling over 500 locos, being used on almost any type of traffic. No. 47100 would be scrapped by Booth Roe Metals, Rotherham, in 1994, although one cab survives at the Ribble Steam Railway.

47109 21 April 1978

No. 47109 (D1697) passes Washwood Heath with a rake of empty Motorail car-carrying wagons. These wagons were attached to long-distance trains to carry cars, again something that has disappeared from the network. No. 47109 was scrapped by MC Metals, Glasgow, in 1989.

47255 19 July 1977

No. 47255 (D1933, 47596) is seen on one of the through roads at York. This loco was allocated to Stratford depot at the time, as seen by the silver roof. Stratford was one of the first depots to personalise its locos and to move away from the corporate all-over blue livery by painting their locos with silver roofs. No. 47255 was eventually refurbished and fitted with eth equipment, being renumbered 47596 in the process, and was preserved at the Mid Norfolk Railway.

47266 26 May 1981

No. 47266 (D1966, 47629, 47828) is seen waiting to depart from Lawley Street container terminal with a loaded working. This loco had not long been released from overhaul at Crewe; including a repaint into standard BR blue livery. This loco still survives today, numbered 47828, and has been preserved at the Dartmoor Railway.

47321 28 June 1984

No. 47321 (D1802) is seen passing Saltley depot, with a rake of withdrawn Class 414 2 HAP EMU units. The EMU cars are boarded up due to asbestos, and are on their way to Vic Berry's yard at Leicester for scrapping. No. 47321 would itself be scrapped by Booth Roe Metals, Rotherham, in 1998.

47370 27 July 1980

No. 47370 (D1889) is seen stabled for the weekend at Immingham depot, Humberside. This particular loco was fitted with an early type of multiple working equipment that was only fitted to this loco and No. 47379. No. 47370 would eventually be scrapped by T. J. Thompson, Stockton, in 2009.

47404 24 August 1984

No. 47404 (D1503) waits departure from Leeds with a northbound working. This loco carries the name *Hadrian*, and was one of the original Class 47s known as generators. Most of these early Class 47s were the first Class 47s withdrawn due to their non-standard equipment. No. 47404 was scrapped by Vic Berry, Leicester, in 1990.

47447 12 August 1976

No. 47447 (D1564) arrives at Rhyl with an express passenger working. Of note is the first carriage, a Mk2 BFK – there being less than 150 of this type of carriage built. No. 47447 has had its headcode wound back to 0000, and it would eventually be scrapped by Booth Roe Metals, Rotherham, in 1994.

47467 17 May 1980

No. 47467 (D1593) is seen at Derby station awaiting departure time. Note how the driver is giving his windscreen a good clean before he departs. No. 47467 has not long been through Crewe Works, judging by the paintwork, and was allocated to Eastfield depot, Glasgow, at the time. No. 47467 was scrapped by EWS at Wigan CRDC in 2000.

47508 28 June 1979

No. 47508 (D1952) *Great Britain* is seen at Exeter St Davids with a parcels working. This had only been named three months previous, and it still looked in a very respectable condition at the time of the shot. No. 47508 would spend its entire career on the Western Region, apart from two years spent at Crewe, before finally being scrapped at Bristol Bath Road in 1995.

47510 17 February 1984

No. 47510 (D1954, 47713) is seen stabled in the snow at Saltley depot, Birmingham. This loco carries the name *Fair Rosamund* and was chosen to be refurbished as a Scottish-based push/pull-fitted Class 47, being renumbered 47713. It was withdrawn following fire damage and was scrapped by Vic Berry, Leicester, in 1990.

47511 21 December 1979

No. 47511 (D1955, 47714) *Thames* is seen stabled at Saltley with slightly larger than normal running numbers. This was another loco selected to be refurbished for the Scottish Region, becoming No. 47714 in the process. This loco is still in use today, as a shunt loco at the Old Dalby test track.

47524 21 April 1984

No. 47524 (D1107) is seen stabled at York stabling point. There were always quite a few locos to be found stabled at York, and they were stabled just down from the National Railway Museum. No. 47524 would eventually find its way into preservation and is today based on the Churnet Valley Railway.

47533 31 July 1982

No. 47533 (D1651) is seen at Birmingham New Street having just uncoupled from a passenger working. Note the old postal Brutes on the platform – an ideal seat for watching the day's activities. No. 47533 would eventually be withdrawn with collision damage it received at Reading, after colliding with No. 47472, and was scrapped at Old Oak Common in 1995.

47538 25 July 1975

No. 47538 (D1669, 968035) is seen waiting to depart from Birmingham New Street with 1Z77. The 'Z' was only used for special workings. When this loco was withdrawn, it was sent to Crewe Works for scrapping, but it was then taken over by the departmental sector for transporting engines from Crewe Works to Crewe depot. This role was to finish in 1995, and the loco was scrapped at Crewe Works in 1997.

47583 22 March 1981

No. 47583 (D1767, 47172, 47734) is seen at Norwich, waiting to depart with an express working to London Liverpool Street. This had only been renumbered from No. 47172 four months previous, and it is seen carrying the name *County of Hertfordshire* and a silver roof, courtesy of its home depot of Stratford. No. 47583 was later renumbered 47734.

47594 25 October 1983

No. 47594 (D1615, 47035, 47739) is seen powering away from a signal check at Witton in the West Midlands while heading for Birmingham New Street. This had been refurbished at Crewe Works just two months previously, which included being renumbered from 47035. It would go on to be renumbered 47739, and is today still in use with Colas Rail Freight.

47901 1 August 1981

No. 47901 (D1628, 47046, 47601) is seen outside the fuel shed at Swindon. This loco was unique in the Class 47 fleet, as it was used as a test bed for the Class 56 engines, and also for the Class 58 engines. It was based around Westbury for use on stone and aggregate traffic, before finally being scrapped by MC Metals, Glasgow, in 1992.

50002 17 May 1981

No. 50002 (D402) is seen at Saltley depot in un-refurbished condition. This loco carries the name *Superb*, and is today preserved at the South Devon Railway.

50047 3 June 1980

No. 50047 (D447) Swiftsure is seen stabled at Saltley depot, Birmingham. By this time the loco had been fully refurbished at Doncaster Works, the tell-tale sign being the headlight fitted to the front, and also the step in the roof being plated over. No. 50047 would be scrapped by Vic Berry, Leicester, in 1989.

55002 19 July 1977

No. 55002 (D9002) is seen departing from York station with a northbound passenger working. This loco carries the name *The Kings Own Yorkshire Light Infantry*, and would be repainted back into BR green livery for its final year in service, before being preserved at the National Railway Museum.

55003 13 April 1980

No. 55003 (D9003) *Meld* is seen standing outside the shed at Finsbury Park, North London. This depot was responsible for maintaining the East Coast fleet of Class 55s at the southern end of the route. This was another London depot that personalised its locos, with the addition of the white window surrounds. No. 55003 was scrapped at Doncaster Works in 1981.

55008 13 April 1980

No. 55008 (D9008) is seen on the fuel road at Finsbury Park depot, North London. These magnificent locomotives were eventually replaced on the East Coast route by the High Speed Trains, and all were withdrawn by 1982. No. 55008 carries the name *The Green Howards* and was scrapped at Doncaster Works in 1982, although one cab survives at Barrow Hill.

55011 13 April 1980

No. 55011 (D9011) *The Royal Northumberland Fusiliers* is seen stabled at Finsbury Park depot. This was allocated to Gateshead depot, near Newcastle at the time, and carries the depot's crest above the running number. The Deltic locos were named after either regiments or famous racehorses. No. 55011 was scrapped at Doncaster Works in 1982.

55014 1 March 1981

No. 55014 (D9014) *The Duke of Wellington's Regiment* is seen inside Doncaster Works awaiting repairs. This loco would be withdrawn at the end of the year, with the last Class 55 taken out of service in January 1982; No. 55014, like the majority of the class, was scrapped at Doncaster in 1982.

56009 2 April 1984

No. 56009 (56201) is seen stabled at Saltley depot Birmingham. This was one of the locos built in Romania, with the class being mainly used for coal traffic, based around the large coalfields of Yorkshire. No. 56009 was eventually taken to Brush at Loughborough as an engine transporter, but has since been moved to the Battlefield Line, carrying the number 56201.

56012 27 July 1980

No. 56012 stands outside Doncaster depot – another notoriously difficult depot to gain access to, and indeed a depot I have never managed to visit. No. 56012 is another Romanian-built example, and it was scrapped at Immingham depot in 2000.

56029 4 April 1980

No. 56029 is seen stabled at Saltley depot, Birmingham, in front of the depot's re-railing coaches. Class 56s were common visitors to Saltley, with the large amount of coal traffic in the area. No. 56029 would be scrapped by European Metal Recycling, Kingsbury, in 2007.

56035 21 April 1978

No. 56035 passes Washwood Heath with a light engine move towards Saltley depot. This loco was only six months old at the time, being one of the first handful of the class to be built at Doncaster. No. 56035 would be scrapped by EWS at Wigan CRDC in 2000.

56041 15 June 1980

No. 56041 is seen stabled for the weekend at Margam depot, South Wales. The South Wales-based Class 56s initially took over the heavy iron ore workings to Llanwern from the triple-headed Class 37s, working in pairs. No. 56041 was scrapped by European Metal Recycling, Attercliffe, in 2011.

56049 10 February 1980

No. 56049 is seen stabled at Saltley depot. Despite the loco being less than two years old, the builder's plate is already missing from the cabside. No. 56049 is still operational today, working for Colas Rail Freight.

56065 10 August 1982

No. 56065 passes Water Orton with a loaded MGR coal working bound for Didcot Power Station. There was a constant flow of coal workings around the Midlands, with traffic to Didcot and Ironbridge. No. 56065 is today stored at Leicester.

56074 24 August 1983

No. 56074 *Kellingley Colliery* is seen passing through Doncaster station with an empty MGR working. Of note on the loco is the orange warning light on the cab roof, only fitted to this loco and No. 56073. No. 56074 would be scrapped by Ron Hull, Rotherham, in 2014.

71014 4 April 1976

No. 71014 (E5014) is seen stabled at Ashford. This class of loco were able to run off both AC current with the pantograph, and also DC current with the pick-up shoes on the bogies. There were twenty-four locos built, of which ten were rebuilt as Class 74 locomotives. No. 71014 would be scrapped at Doncaster Works in 1979.

73001 4 April 1976

No. 73001 (E6001, 73901) is seen stabled outside the shed at Hither Green depot, London. This was the very first Class 73 built, and one of only six in the Class 73/0 subclass. It would later be preserved, and is today based at the Dean Forest Railway.

73106 23 May 1985

No. 73106 (E6012) is seen stabled at Saltley depot, Birmingham. These locos were incredibly rare visitors to the Midlands at this time; this had worked up to the area on a freight working, only to be hurriedly sent back south. No. 73106 was scrapped by Booth Roe Metals, Rotherham, in 2004.

73118 23 March 1985

No. 73118 (E6024) is seen stabled at Clapham Junction in front of an observation saloon. This loco would eventually be fitted with a Scharfenberg coupling, enabling it to couple-up to Class 373 Eurostar EMUs. It was later withdrawn, and is now preserved at the Vale of Glamorgan Railway, Barry.

73121 23 March 1985

No. 73121 (E6028, 73208, 73965) *Croydon 1883 – 1983* is seen stabled at Clapham Junction at the head of a rake of parcels vans. The Southern Region always took great pride in naming their locomotives, often fitting them with crests above or below the nameplate. No. 73121 is still in use today – although it has been renumbered 73965 – and works for GBRf.

73129 4 April 1976

No. 73129 (E6036) is seen stabled outside the refuelling shed at Hither Green depot. This was another Class 73 to be preserved, and is now based on the Gloucestershire & Warwickshire Railway.

73131 10 October 1981

No. 73131 (E6038) is seen at Bournemouth station with a passenger working. This loco would be scrapped by C. F. Booth, Rotherham, in 2004.

73135 3 April 1976

No. 73135 (E6042, 73235) is seen stabled in the spring sunshine at Brighton. The Class 73 locomotives were all based on the Southern Region at this time, but today they can be found further afield. No. 73135 would be renumbered 73235 for Gatwick Express duties, and is today based at Bournemouth depot as a shunt loco.

74004 3 April 1976

No. 74004 (E5000, E5024, E6104) is seen outside Eastleigh Works following overhaul, including a fresh coat of BR blue livery. This was the pioneer Class 71 loco, and was rebuilt as No. 74004 at Doncaster in 1968. It would be scrapped by Birds at Long Marston in 1978.

76010 14 March 1976

No. 76010 (E26010) is seen stabled at Reddish depot, near Manchester. This class of loco was only ever used on the Woodhead route, due to its different voltage, and when the line closed the whole class was withdrawn. No. 76010 was scrapped by C. F. Booth Rotherham in 1983.

81007 31 August 1984

No. 81007 (E3008) is seen at Crewe station, waiting for the road to depart. There were twenty-five of these locomotives built at the Birmingham Railway Carriage & Wagon Company, Smethwick, although three members of the class were scrapped before they received their TOPS numbers. No. 81007 would be scrapped by Coopers Metals, Sheffield, in 1992.

82001 9 November 1980

No. 82001 (E3047) is seen outside Crewe Works awaiting attention. Crewe undertook all the overhauls on the AC electric fleet at this time. No. 82001 was scrapped by Vic Berry, Leicester, in 1985.

83015 23 March 1985

No. 83015 (E3100) is seen at London Euston. By this time the loco was employed on ECS duties between Euston and Wembley carriage sidings, and looked superb retaining its domino headcode panel. It would be scrapped by MC Metals, Glasgow, in 1993.

84004 14 March 1976

No. 84004 (E3039) is seen stabled outside Allerton depot, Liverpool. There were only ten of this class built by North British, and they were all withdrawn by 1980, with No. 84004 being scrapped by Birds, Long Marston, in 1985.

84008 9 November 1980

No. 84008 (E3043) is seen withdrawn at Crewe Works. Amazingly, this loco would survive for another eight years before being scrapped in 1988 at Crewe.

85003 31 August 1984

No. 85003 (E3058, 85113) is seen double-heading the Crewe Works test train through Crewe while coupled with No. 85023. No. 85003 would eventually be renumbered 85113, and would be scrapped by MC Metals, Glasgow, in 1993.

85017 17 May 1981

No. 85017 (E3072) is seen stabled outside Tyseley depot, Birmingham. This depot was responsible for the West Midlands DMU fleet, and was not electrified, but electric locos did visit for repairs. No. 85017 would be scrapped by MC Metals, Glasgow, in 1993, after suffering fire damage near Berkswell.

85022 3 April 1985

No. 85022 (E3077) is seen making a station call at Nuneaton with a rake of Mk1 carriages. At this time the Class 85s were still employed on express passenger work, up until the introduction of the Class 90s. No. 85022 would be scrapped by MC Metals, Glasgow, in 1993.

85025 23 March 1985

No. 85025 (E3080) is seen awaiting departure time from London Euston with an express passenger working. No. 85025 would be one of a handful of the class that were scrapped by Vic Berry, Leicester, in 1991.

85026 3 April 1985

No. 85026 (E3081) is seen stabled at Nuneaton. This view has changed considerably, with the lines the loco sits on having been removed and a new platform in their place leading to the flyover at the north end of the station. No. 85026 was scrapped by MC Metals, Glasgow, in 1993.

86008 25 July 1975

No. 86008 (E3180, 86408, 86608, 86501) is seen stabled on one of the through roads at Birmingham New Street. This loco still survives today, renumbered as 86608 and working for Freightliner.

86235 18 August 1980

No. 86235 (E3194) *Novelty* is seen at Vauxhall carriage sidings, Birmingham. The loco carries a special livery in connection with the 150th anniversary of the Liverpool to Manchester Railway. No. 86235 has recently been exported to Bulgaria, working for Bulmarket.

87004 31 August 1973

No. 87004 departs Birmingham New Street with a passenger working to London Euston. This loco was only one month old at the time, and carries its running number on both cabsides. No. 87004 would eventually be exported to Bulgaria, working for BZK.

87010 20 August 1974

No. 87010 is seen waiting departure time at Birmingham New Street with a working to London Euston. No. 87010 would be another member of the class exported to Bulgaria, working for BZK.

97202 11 February 1984

No. 97202 (D5281, 25131) is seen stabled at Toton depot, Nottinghamshire. This had been renumbered from 25131 for departmental duties, but was eventually sent to Vic Berry, Leicester, in 1987 for scrapping.

53007 20 April 1984

No. 53007 (50007) departs Doncaster in typically smoky fashion. During this time, British Rail painted the vast majority of its units and coaching stock into the attractive blue and grey livery to compliment the blue livery of its locomotives. No. 53007 would eventually be scrapped by Mayer Newman, Snailwell, in 1988.

56012 1 March 1981

No. 56012 (54012) rests in the dock platform at the south end of Doncaster Station, before departing for Sheffield. Of note are the First Class section and the South Yorkshire emblem. No. 56012 was eventually renumbered No. 54012 and was scrapped by Mayer Newman, Snailwell, in 1991.

303066 10 August 1982

No. 303066 is seen stabled in one of the bays at the south end of Rugby station. This class of EMU were built for suburban services around Glasgow, but a few moved south to Longsight for use around Manchester. No. 303066 would be scrapped by Mayer Parry, Snailwell, in 1991.

304022 23 May 1982

No. 304022 is seen stabled at Cockshute sidings, Stoke-on-Trent, for the weekend. At this time, No. 304022 still carried plain blue livery, and was one of forty-five Class 304 units operated by the London Midland Region. No. 304022 would be scrapped by Vic Berry, Leicester, in 1985, by which time it had received blue and grey livery.

312202 10 August 1982

No. 312202 (312728) stands on the sidings adjacent to Rugby Station. The London Midland Region had four of these units allocated, and all would eventually be transferred away to East Ham, with No. 312202 being renumbered 312728 while it was allocated down south. No. 312728 would be scrapped by Sims Metals, Newport, in 2005.

28355 14 March 1975

No. 28355 is seen waiting to depart from Southport. This class of unit were designated as Class 502 units, and all were based on the 650v DC third rail lines around Liverpool. No. 28355 was built in 1940 by the LMS at their Derby works, and would be scrapped by Mayer Newman, Snailwell, in 1980.

29147 8 February 1981

No. 29147 is seen outside Horwich Works following overhaul, and a repaint into blue and grey livery. This class of unit were the Class 503s, and they too were allocated to the 650v DC system in Liverpool. No. 29147 was built by the Birmingham Railway Carriage & Wagon Company, Smethwick in 1956, and was scrapped by Vic Berry, at Northwich, in 1985.

59605 8 February 1981

No. 59605 is seen outside Horwich Works following overhaul, and repaint. This unit was one of just eight three-car units ordered by the LNER for use on the 1500v DC Woodhead route, and also to Hadfield. They didn't enter service until 1954, and all were withdrawn following the closure of the Woodhead route, and the conversion of the Hadfield route to 25kv operation in 1984. No. 59605 was scrapped by C. F. Booth, Rotherham, in 1985.